Jean Claude Pondevie
Soft-Tech Architecture

Texts by
Mario Antonio Arnaboldi

l'ARCAEDIZIONI

Photographic Credits
Jean Claude Pondevie
Philippe Ruault
Société Vittuel

Editorial Director USA
Pierantonio Giacoppo

Chief Editor of Collection
Maurizio Vitta

Publishing Coordinator
Franca Rottola

Graphic Design
ST Graphic

Translation
James Pallas

Editing
Martin J. Anderson

Colour-separation
Litofilms Italia, Bergamo

Printing
Poligrafiche Bolis, Bergamo

First published March 1999

ISBN 88-7838-074-1

Contents

Functionalism or no Functionalism

by Mario Antonio Arnaboldi

At last we have a French architect capable of sending out a "signal of contemporaneity". The architect in question is Jean-Claude Pondevie, who set up his own firm in Nantes a number of years ago, turning a deaf ear to "romantic" architecture, the architecture favoured by the Solons of our day. Instead, he successfully geared his projects to an architectonic discourse rich in new symbols, thereby displaying an uncanny mastery of a stylistic idiom under the banner of functionalism. Professionalism and a passion for architecture drove Pondevie to build private houses, public buildings, schools, media-libraries, and hospitals designed with great precision and rigour. All his works are based on a careful choice of materials that allow architecture to exploit the geometrical force of functionalism, without making his designs look like functionalist projects. Even the contents of the underlying ideas behind his works, with their multifunctional designs linked to life and leisure, are geared to their images. Pondevie's works of architecture are actually nothing less than a shrine to "intelligent" living. Many of his works look high-spirited owing to the austere way in which they are situated in the landscape.

They never betray the strong presence of functionalism in the surroundings, but they manage to express great communicative force and power of attraction. At least we have a new form architecture in the midst of many other rather unhappy works of architecture of a functionalist tendency which, for the most part, lack both courage and expressive force. One reason for all this may be our universities, which, all too often, just teach students to copy what has already been done; that is to say, teach them to imitate existing works of architecture. Taking what these teachers say to the letter - frightened, as they are, of even the word "creativity" - is a widespread illness among the younger generations. To have the courage to express one's personal thoughts, confident in one's own knowledge and the future of architectural design is, on the contrary, a rare thing. This is why Jean-Claude Pondevie's architectural firm has attracted the attention of the critics and of those who for years have been defending, within the educational system, this way of being contemporary, to the detriment of all those who want nothing more than mediocrity and desolation.

This lack of creativity is synonymous with "poverty", cultural poverty, lack of courage and personality. We are grateful to professionals like Pondevie, who have imposed their work with such clarity, through projects carried out with such meticulous care. But we need to make a few brief references to architecture in general in order to grasp certain side-effects blocking the development of this new evolution in architectonic forms. It is the difficult relationship between architecture and politics, particularly evident in France in recent years, that brings to the surface only a vague idea of the difficulties involved in territorial control.

There is no true laboratory for building design, something that once existed in all large cities; there is also an increasing lack of "intelligent" clients. Pondevie is striving to overcome these drawbacks and to identify with a particular style capable of guaranteeing the kind of cultural continuity which is intrinsic to architectural design. The ups-and-downs of architecture intertwine with philosophical discussions that tend to anticipate and dictate the kind of environment in which we live in the future.

This is not just a descriptive of a possible state of affairs, since all the technological means at our disposal for operating on a habitat form an art: an art produced by the "creators of the city", whose work justifies and injects meaning into design. Pondevie's various projects, as places full of life where careful attention is paid to the body and to public functions (i.e. meeting places), are integral parts of the new architectural design, since they seem to be technological developments and, at the same time, appeals to the memory, and to consolidated typological styles. Shaping architecture through its materials and supports is one of the natural components of architectural space; it is the usual way to leave a trace not only on the world that surrounds us but also on ourselves and on time. Pondevie tries this experiment and uses white plaster as the perceptual structure of his design spaces, which turns into decoration, texture, and form, creating fascinating results. At times it almost seems an impossible task to modify human behaviour through architectural form and leave a mark on history; but there can be no doubting that this French architect has succeeded in this intent. Contemporary architecture is capable of retracing the path left behind by the Masters of our profession and of reviving interest in the search for new signs capable of creating new styles: and this is precisely where Pondevie has succeeded.

Irrational Functionalism in Small Dones

Schools of architecture spread their messages across the various continents of the globe. To speak of projects carried out in France now means to speak of architectural experiments in relation to the whole world: this is the real meaning that should be given to "total architecture"; it means to speak in concrete terms of Marshall McLuhan's global village, or of "little meetings" designed for the purposes of communication, that lead to immediate encounters across great distances.

Jean-Claude Pondevie, having graduated from the Institut d'Urbanisme at the University of Paris, began his professional career in Nantes, in a region of France where tradition merges with the agricultural world, with the ancient Celts, the Namnetes, and the Huguenots; a melting-pot of tradition in a place where industrial-agricultural production provide a perfect example of quality. And so we have his project for a "Tree House", entitled "La Folie Finfarine", built in La Poiroux in 1995 or his "Espace Culturel" at Aizenay dating back to 1990, both of which physically embody his philosophy of design. It is perhaps worthwhile making a few remarks about his architectural work as a whole.

The places chosen for constructing his works of architecture are, for the most part, situated on the outskirts of cities, and, generally speaking, they overlook rivers or motorways, like the Route de Maché or the Route de Challans, as in the case of the "Espace Culturel" project, thereby offering various architectural solutions that change in relation to the various means of access and points of view. As regards this project in particular, the roads for vehicles, pedestrians, and the entrance way to the theatre, are the real guidelines around which the architectural design has been created.

These quick references to his

approach to design help us to understand the powerful impact his work has on the surrounding environment in general. But to fully appreciate the importance of Pondevie's artistry in creating his architecture and to begin to understand the cultural depth of his works, we need to gauge the idiomatic references he uses to design these spaces. It is always difficult to impose a relation between man and nature; but it is just as difficult to think of the kind of relation that exists between everyday life and surrounding nature.

Architecture sometimes, with time, manages to transform the way it interacts with such a violently evolving force as nature. This, then, is the underlying theme, this is how Pondevie has interpreted the powerful impact between the elements that dictate architectural design and the people who inhabit its works. Pondevie had no doubts about adopting a rational approach, based entirely on Euclidean mathematics, that embodies a feeling of certainty about our way of living.

Up to now the geometrical forms of functionalism, which, as Alberto Sartoris used to say, are the most deeply rooted and strongest, have made it possible to identify man's most intricate certainties and, above all, the expressions of his work. Two entities are now clearly brought to the fore: nature and the individual. To live and work around the Loire, particularly today, might

perhaps mean to embrace the rationalism of Leon Battista Alberti's well-known golden section, in the sense of the need for some certainty in life. And then the materials that form Pondevie's architecture almost always appear to be a fitting confirmation of the entire design process. They are evidence of worked material, manipulated with the same geometrical forms of logic that dictated the whole operation. The design phases gradually take shape, the thought behind the project flows along with well-articulated forms on the inside and the architectural space manages in this way to project itself outside with efficacy and strength.

There are also moments of lyricism when, for example, the glass and occasionally curved surfaces appear through other architectural facades, designed in careful geometric or curving forms. His works almost always tend to compete with the surrounding nature and with the presence of man and his way of feeling and being. It is as if Pondevie expressed visual and perceptual certainties, with which he then deforms the way we take in the environment. He almost always manages to describe a piece of France and his way of perceiving it. Architecture possesses this magic; and if it is well constructed, it has the strength to make us reflect on the materials manipulated by man. This takes place through the air of his space and the light that describes its

outline. Pondevie shows that he has taken great care over writing his architectural narratives, and, in actual fact, he seems to have had no doubts about his choice of idiom and the distributive logic of his forms. All this shows that architecture is now turning its gaze in other directions and is looking for greater participation in new forms capable of pulling it away from a past which is beginning to weigh heavily on the present.

Pondevie does not seem to want to address emerging trends in architectural design, but he takes great care over choosing the contexts in which his projects are located: he treats the surroundings as a strong and dramatically involving element. In these values of functionalism he almost always wants to find the kind of expressive artistry that has marked the great architectural events of the past. Pondevie insists on this, with a trembling rhythm of assonances, without seeking any form of transgression: his certainty is fascinating.

Organic Synthesis
Contemporary architecture must humanise the product of man's work, which is the fruit of an intellectual act on the part of man, and must put it concretely at his service, so as to celebrate, through events, utility and beauty.

Jean-Claude Pondevie really seems to have worked in this direction, putting the project at the centre of his painstaking search for a synthesis of the organic, for a means of bringing together space and idiom. In general his work sums up the maturity he reached in his constructions, which are often dense with suggestive signals. Once terminated, the work that he foresaw while still at the planning stage becomes even more evident: Pondevie's organic design gives a sense of continuity to architecture. In fact, it is by retracing his steps that we can best understand the path of a leading exponent of contemporary architecture who tends to fight "Post-Modernism", which is not only confused and futile but also intrinsically sterile. This struggle shows up not only in his projects but also in those of other contemporaries: take, for instance, the plastic force with which he designed the spaces of the "Maison Thoulouzan" at La Faute sur Mer, built in 1991, to mention just one of his projects. In general his work has been instrumental in lowering the credibility of certain post-modern critics who would have people believe that modern architecture is dead.

Today, now that even the false certainties of the International Style have broken down, there seems to be a renewed interest in approaches and standards of organic architecture that has so often left its mark on the history of our profession. Jean-Claude Pondevie, now a sincere and open supporter of the organic cause in architecture, has contrived to become a powerful promoter of the roots of the organic vision and has been speaking with increasing hostility about the dogmas of classicism, knowing full well that space, in itself, is the real protagonist of architecture. He has managed to change the viewpoint on architectural design in general, by changing the terms of its results; through his works he has come to represent a new understanding of architectural space, as kinetic energy useful for its transformation. This enables him to obtain, through the use of his white walls, a higher and higher level of architectural quality.

All this comes out in studying the stylistic definition given to the "Lycée Professionel Valère Mathé" at Olonne sur Mer, designed by Pondevie in 1992. An even more extensive confirmation will be found in his project for the "Médiathèque" at Saint Herblain, designed in 1991, in which painted steel and glass are wed in a sophisticated and delicate composition. It is the use to which the materials are put, as can already be seen in the design phase, that delimits the creative field of the project; it documents on the physical aspect and working of the materials, characterising functionalist architecture.

The continual experimentation carried out by Pondevie is therefore aimed at the forces of interior space which come together in the way of representing space from the exterior, at the tensile forces of materials, and at the forces of perception which, by way of the mind, fascinate the observer. One last force that brings them all to a close is the syntax with which his architecture is able to express phrases denoting organic qualities and new numbers, riches that drive him towards continual innovation of his projects. Architecture - real architecture, that is - is an act that looks to the future, and it is therefore a "young" act for designers who want to eliminate any form of academic repetitiveness.

It is the works of architecture designed by the great masters and by those, like Pondevie, who follow their school, that bring us back to the great subjects of modernity. Confused debate on Postmodernism has had surprising results: far from throwing any light on this term, it has convinced us that we even have confused ideas about the term that logically and chronologically precedes it: "modern".

The questions posed are: when did modernity begin, how far does it extend, and what is its consistency? The debate between the romantics who have discovered a form of architecture already invented and academically repetitious, and those who instead believe in the new and have glimpsed an evolution in design that passes through organic architecture, is what might lead to a new style. The science of numbers, the new way of interpreting organic reality, makes us feel closer to nature and perhaps more desirous of spaces of tension designed to boost our vitality, filling us with both amazement and pleasure. This is the way that the moderns clear out their mental stockrooms: they do so in such a way that inside there is still some room to make headway. From this comes the idea, which is absolutely central to modernity, of progress, a term which is to be taken literally, as the possibility of moving directly ahead without setting any limits; it is this that Jean-Claude Pondevie's work helps us to understand.

Meticulous Organisation

Jean-Claude Pondevie shows meticulous organization and great design expertise in working on the precise and subtle themes of contemporary living, especially those themes of great topical interest. Pondevie fits into the ranks of the likes of Terragni, Figini and Pollini, Le Corbusier and Gropius but, in a more specific way, he is more attentive to the traditions of French architecture in the twenties. In fact, he is constantly on the lookout for any sign capable of offering an opportunity for the impulses generated by a sense of place.

By doing so he contrives to make his architecture an archetype for the city. In this way, through his work as an architect, Pondevie takes up this signal and, in line with local tradition, finds the logical forms that govern the images of his project, to the point of recognizing its operational relevance especially in the Loire with its great cultural heritage. In many of his projects, the French countryside becomes dense with meanings, owing to Pondevie's curiosity about history, the hinterland and the peculiar traditions of this strip of French soil. It is not only the wealth brought by work but, above all, the faith and the craftsmanship innate in the local people that Pondevie refers to. It is as if it were the style of a part of France that has always competed in a rigorous economy of art and exchange.

Consequently, designing in harmony with this type of logic means turning a cultural tradition to "stone". Pondevie carries out the task of singling out and experimenting into the connotations of these character-instilling phenomena, and he translates them into the formal indices of his projects. He softens his forms, however, in the current style of advanced technology which is now standardizing the architectural appearance of so many contemporary projects, making them all look more or less the same.

In this post-functionalist context Pondevie is particularly creative, to the point of making the success of his ideas depend on his personal skills, thereby making himself responsible for their being carried out. It is the correctness of his experimentation and his style which, with their characteristics and merits, play a decisive role in the design work of his firm. Jean-Claude Pondevie's merit lies in his humanity, even more than in his technical knowledge of design.

He is able to establish a creative atmosphere in his firm, and this is the fundamental point to which all other organizational problems are subordinated. There is nothing more mortifying to the vitality of design than repetitious work, which inevitably ends up stiffening one's mental reflexes. In the context of his work this is the reason why his projects look like some new methodology of planning, like something that can stand by itself, in which a balance has been struck between the man himself and the force of his architectural design. His art, his expertise, the design and "atmosphere" of creative tension, are his contribution to the future of his design. Pondevie knows, however, that the contribution of culture and the hinterland of France cannot develop and spread any faster than the society that he means to celebrate. In fact, treated in this way, traditional architecture, made of simple forms, broad dimensions, and contrasts, becomes almost "dramatic". This is why Pondevie's works even contain the essence of the antiquity of the Namnetes.

Technology + Art = Innovation

It becomes quite spontaneous, then, to pause to consider Pondevie's tireless dedication to architectural competitions and his quiet way of expressing architectural designs capable of offering rigorous, balanced and rational groundings to architectural art.

This, however, is not sufficient, nor is the design machine set up by Pondevie and his expert technicians, working together to build one of his works of architecture. It is not sufficient, but, without a doubt, it is necessary, if the building material is to contain architecture's transformational force, which above all calls for decision-makers. This is meant as a comment on those who, having the power to decide, want to transform the territory so that it provides a constructive service for man. Offering suitable services through an event is what makes the improvement of its quality a future possibility. When the person who makes decisions, in political and economic terms, regarding our future, intends concretely to build a work of architecture, and when someone who takes upon himself the right to manage our future and has the real will to do so and not to speculate politically, he shows that he really appreciates the true values of architecture. This is the moment of truth, and the time that puts the event face to face with history. In other words, it involves realising that mankind has grown and needs great works in order to assert man's rights over nature and the future of the human spirit. The premonitory signs of man's growth take their place among the great values of the

spirit and call for confirmation in the facts that link the house of man and nature. Man and society are moving into such a determined future that they can no longer pause and dwell only on the signals of the past, so they tend to discover everything that matter and the numbers that govern it can make tangible.

The picture of these values takes shape in reading about everything that came before us in the world of design, not in the way in which it was written. The Machu Picchu charter issued in 1997 has modified and integrated the rationalist charter of Athens dictated by Le Corbusier in 1933. Pluralism and complexity then took over.

Today, planning requires systematic interaction among planners, clients and administrators. Ignoring this fact will only result in a great waste of economic and intellectual resources - that is, it is only an indication of rebellion on the part of active "culture". The positions that emerged from the Biennial of Venice in 1980 found few followers, who expressed themselves in outdated, eclectic, and evasive forms that smacked of their romantic and academic origins. Since the time of the Athens Charter, the population has doubled, creating the crises that are undermining contemporary society. The Modern Movement is preparing for the next century with solid victories over the academic world and its symmetrical

architecture of finished forms.

The deconstructivism of Eisenman, Gehry and Libeskind is plainly an agent of insecurity and discord. There re-emerges the "zero degree" of non-vernacular popular architecture. A new pole is born allied with the design purposes of Pondevie, with Meier, Birkerts, Rogers and Pei, a pole no longer simple but sophisticated in its complexity. Here, once again, in a large building we find the perpetuation of carefully gauged values: buildings with public functions become places appointed to represent these wishes, tending towards transformation and based on everything connected with research, mathematics, and the behaviour of materials, all of which is at building's service in the name of intelligent "technology".

A mathematics of values, a rational rule, so accessible as to emanate the spirit of a universal idiom, in a union of common feeling. Pondevie is fighting for this, confident in his certainty that contemporaneity and the modernity of work are the only values to mark out in the territory. Roberto Pane says that "the characteristics so often invoked today, which go by the name of rationality, functionality, and organicity will never be enough by themselves: they must be subordinated to a taste and, whatever their tendency, taste is of an aesthetic nature and not rational". With these words he seems to be defining Pondevie's inspiration in architectural design, which is generally reflected in all his work and particularly in the "Groupe Scolaire - Centre Hospitalier Spécialisé" in La Roche sur Yon, built in 1993.

Transient Simplicity

Completed in 1994, the "Musée du Vignoble du Pays Nantais" at Le Pallet reveals an originality of design that essentially consists in having created a simple exhibition space, enclosed by glass walls equipped with special filters for direct sunlight. All of this is set on a spatial layout which very clearly defines the sequences of exhibition corridors. A special cantilevered roof, which creates a perspective view of the main front, characterizes the building as nothing less than an articulation of connected spaces.

This is the element that best describes the complex on the whole, identifying it with a formal strength so total that it becomes a precise reference point for the territory. The museum contains five rooms housing exhibits of statues, ceramics, and paintings, the arts that generated this discourse on the history and tradition of the French terrain of Nantes. The meaning of this project is that of a museum which builds the whole distributional logic of its exhibition rooms around their contents and surroundings. It is therefore interesting to observe that there is something in the project that describes a simple style which,

though not explicitly stated, determines its historical level. It is its opposition to a "line" of architectural historiography which also, or especially, owing to the prestige of a functionalism of the past, has always strongly emphasized "expressionist" tradition, the "simple style" of which it is precisely the opposite.

This is a battle that has been going on for some time now, and one to which Pondevie's work has made a significant contribution. If this return to functionalist rigour may leave some doubts, they will not be found in the single sharp and probing analyses of constructional details but, actually, in the general assumption of having chosen an ephemeral language to describe what is "simple".

All of Pondevie's works courageously try to define what "simple style" really is, but they leave open a great many possibilities; indeed, the also leave open the wish to understand further forms of logic. Actually, though already known, the concept of ephemeral old work is, and remains, far too general and so vaguely defined that it lends itself to misunderstandings and dubious relationships.

Pondevie clearly gives one the impression of knowing how to distinguish between the values of the ephemeral work of the past and the effect desired in present-day architectural reality. Pondevie then focused on the "simple", as Calvino understood it, in the sense

of natural material; like Dante's panther, which is everywhere and yet dwells nowhere. The project looks as if it approved of "difference" and reveals its continuity, the continuity that is historically acknowledged, as a distinction and not as opposition. Even for describing his whole output with idiomatic compactness, compared with existing architecture, the stylistic idiom of his buildings is as opposed as "open" is to "closed", or "poly" to "monocentric", and so on.

The fundamental fact is that "simple" and "ephemeral", in reference to architecture, are positive notions in the negation of their meaning in the past. "Terseness" and "expressive concentration" are also present in the form with which he designed his project, qualities, moreover, which are not inclusive of simplicity and do not exhaust the concept of "gravitas". In general, then, his projects are, beyond question, discriminating works, an outstanding study which, with great severity, runs counter to "overprecious" and "overexpressive" works. And they most certainly contain many elements of the recent history of architecture.

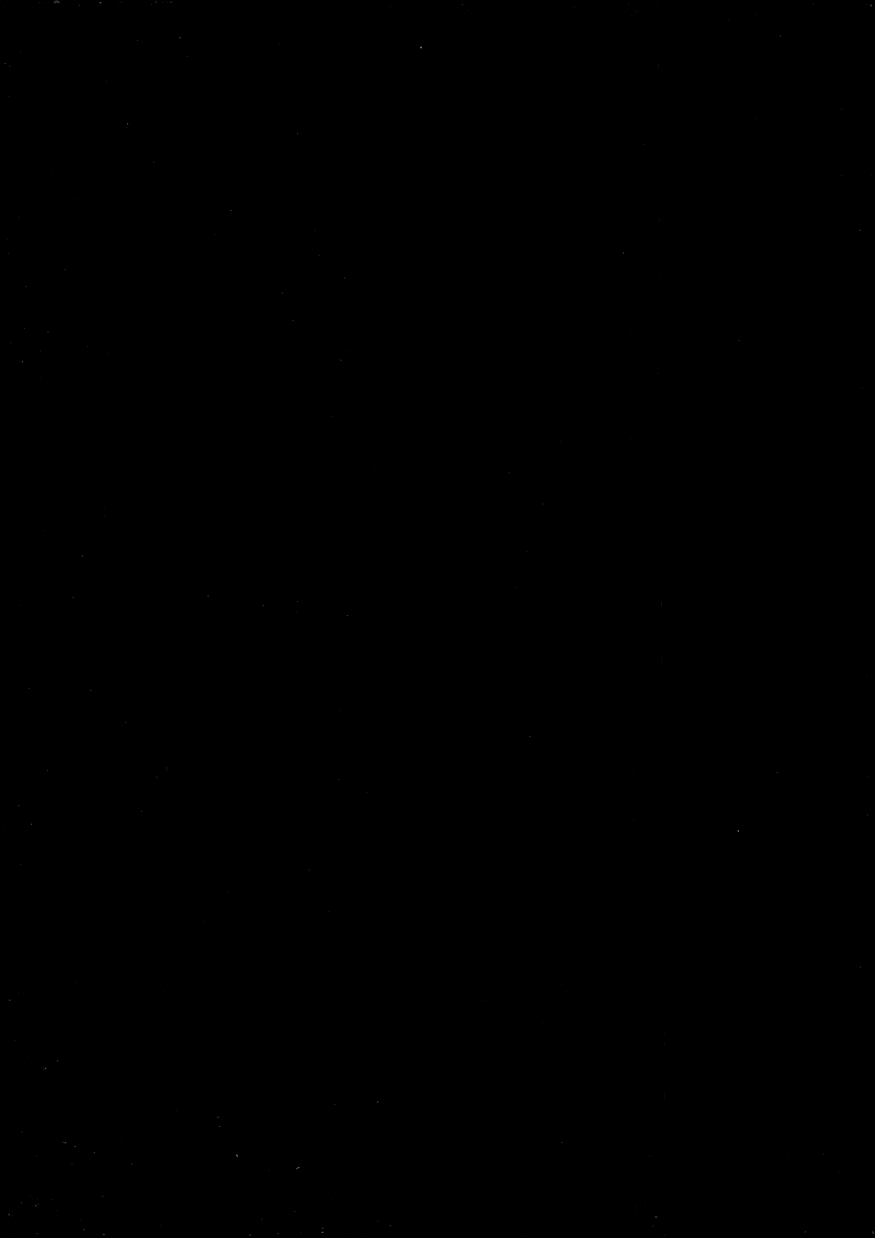

Works

A One-Family House
Le Château d'Olonne, 1989

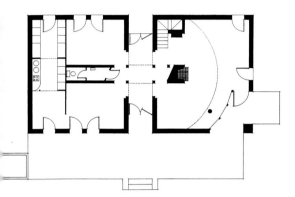

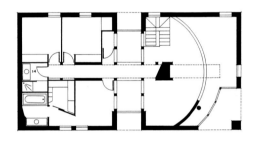

Plan of ground floor.

Top, plan of first floor.
The plans illustrate
the module
of the geometrical
rule as a condition
of architecture.

Not far from the sea at Château d'Olonne, on a building site mainly composed of single villas, Jean-Claude Pondevie built a one-family residence. The architecture of the building reflects the surroundings, and above all, the architecturally "sound" buildings constructed at the end of the nineteenth century. Pondevie's aim was to obtain a definite relationship between he image of this villa and the already existing constructions: but this is a symmetrical relationship, which consists in the use of new materials, like slate and zinc, in a zone dense with sheet-iron roofs, and with exotic vegetation (palm trees and sequoias) among lawns and coppices. Called "*la côte de lumière*", the zone gave the architect the idea for an architectonic structure which is defined by its use of steel, its white walls and the transparency of the glass walls; all of which describes a volume whose predominant orientation is along the east-west axis. Fundamentally, the house follows the main characteristics of the old neighbouring houses reconsidered in a contemporary key. The white-lacquered sheet-iron roofing required accessories in the same tone (the chimney or acroterion); and the facades with their equally white door and window frames, play on the symmetry and dissymmetry of the openings, thereby continually raising an argument about the solemnity of the whole.

Cube, square, and
surface punctuate
architectonic space.

The architectonic whole
of the house.

The detail that
illustrates the
relationship between
form and materials.

The continuity of space between the concave and the convex.

An image of memory between vegetal nature and structural artifice.

The interior becomes the essence of changes in behaviour in the house.

Interior space and the polygonal as the adjustment of a curve become the signs of architectonic discourse.

Above and below meet in the continuity of interior space.

The essentiality of the furnishings underscores the purity of the architectonic sign.

Cultural Centre
Aizenay, 1990

This building is situated on the outskirts of Aizenay, not far from the road for Challans. The basic idea of the project was to define the various public functions that it would have to fulfil, in order to confer a precise architectonic identity on the construction. Access to the building is marked by a

The curve as the suturing element of the facade.

Plan of the Cultural Centre and axonometric vertical section of the whole complex.

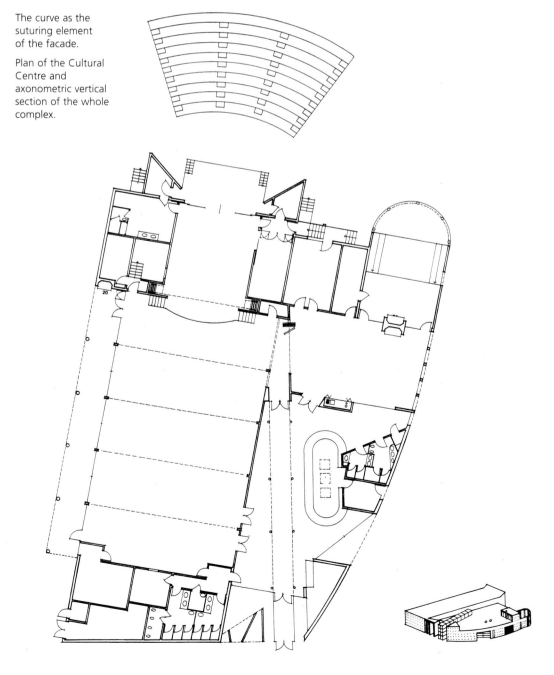

gradual driveway leading from the parking area to the intermediate spaces reserved for outdoor exhibits, a funfair, and so on, up to the real entrance to the Centre, whose curved facade follows the course of the exterior spaces. In the Cultural Centre one finds a large hall reserved for congresses or

theatrical performances, as well as a ticket office and bar, spaces for exhibits, a smaller room, private rooms for restricted meetings, rooms for the administration, and facilities.

Just before the main entrance is a space that, in a way, serves as a filter. It extends as far as the entrance hall, owing to "fault" illuminated from above, which defines the hierarchy of the various functions and of the relative spaces: to the right the ticket office, to the left an exhibition area, to the front on the right, the bar. The main hall can accommodate four hundred people. It is equipped with a false ceiling which, apart from its decorative role, was studied to deal with all the acoustical problems.

The smallest room, which is equipped and used for dancing lessons, lengthens out onto an outer stage, whose oblique walls facilitate the diffusion of the sound. The relationship between the exterior and interior is quite close. The two main halls open on their respective terraces, which are well-provided with greenery. The planner's intention was to emphasize the cultural character of the building: neither a monumental nor a commonplace construction was wanted. Accordingly, Pondevie designed a work which constitutes a very particular presence in the town, a presence underscored by the white painting of the walls, which reflects the colour of many of the houses in the area.

Full view of the Cultural
Centre as seen from
the side and from
the main entrance.

The interior seen
as a continuity
and connection
between the inside
and the outside.

The choice of an architectonic rhythm in the composition of the Cultural Centre.

Thoulouzan House
La Faute sur Mer, 1991

The relationship between the concave and the convex, between flat and curve.

In the pine grove facing the beach of Faute sur Mer in the Vendée, in a building lot recently divided up, Jean-Claude Pondevie efficaciously addresses his basic theme: the integration of a construction with its environment. In this case the natural environment consists of a pine grove and its green facing the sea. Moreover, the urbanization now taking place, thanks to the mediation of the Association Foncière Urbaine of this part of the urban territory, has initiated the construction of mock-rustic houses, and this house was built at the end of the road, in one of the more densely built-up zones in the Amourettes sector, consisting of large lots.

The facade of the construction looking on the road attempts to camouflage itself in the natural environment, and to give the latter a feeling of neutrality, but also of rupture, with respect to the building. But the rear facade, immersed in green, clearly reveals its modernity.

The quarter of a circle on which the plan of the building has been grafted allows the living room to enjoy sunlight for most of the day. The vivid white of the walls, in contrast with the wooden structure of the northern facade and of the terrace, evokes the traditional colour of the residences in this part of the *côte de lumière*.

The geometrical essentiality of the place becomes here relationship, exchange, and connection. Above all, it becomes a work of architecture that brings with it the values of the architectonic culture that since Leon Battista Alberti has characterized western planning.

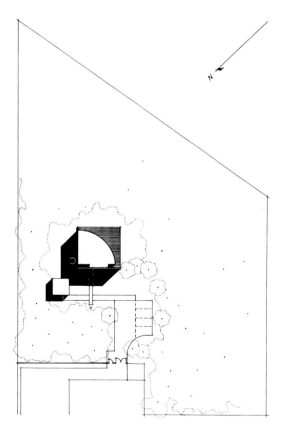

General plan describing the relation between the work of architecture and its surroundings.

The layout
of the ground floor
and the first floor,
in which the rational
essentiality of the form
of the layout becomes
clear.

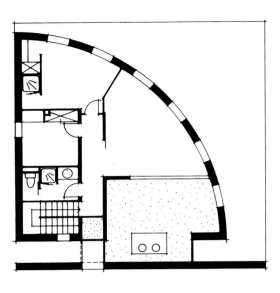

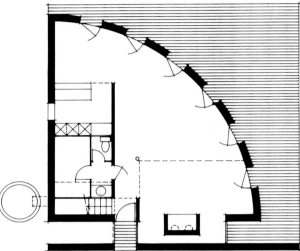

Texture as a comment
on the essentiality of a
plan.

The implosion
of interior space.

The punctuation of the
facade with full and
empty spaces seen from
the main front.

Médiathèque
Saint Herblain, 1991

Jean-Claude Pondevie planned a Médiathèque to be built on a flat meadow on the outskirts of the town of Saint Herblain, organizing it in such a way that the building emerges from the green and is placed in direct relation to the urban agglomerate.

The construction rests on the meadow like a marble sculpture. The almost rectangular layout is traversed diagonally by a corridor designed like a deconstructive gesture with respect to the regularity of the plan. This corridor, off axis with respect to the main facade, gives strength to the whole building, emphasizing its monumental vocation which, in turn, recalls the public function of these spaces.

The cylindrical forms, suggestive of Doric columns and canopies carved to the shape of Renaissance portals, condense the meaning of an architecture destined for public receptions and relations.

The organization of the interior spaces likewise expresses the very highest architectonic values. The library is accessible by way of the parking area. The entrance hall with the facilities looking on it, and the club, can be isolated but they also provide access to the exhibits, from which one can gain access to the spaces reserved for music and reading.

The rooms reserved for the administration offices, the studios, various facilities, and the technical offices are separate from the main volume of the building, but connected by means of a passage.

In this way, this project of Pondevie's is related to the territory and the immediate environment, though fully preserving its individuality.

Sign and design
of the plan at the
moment of intuition.

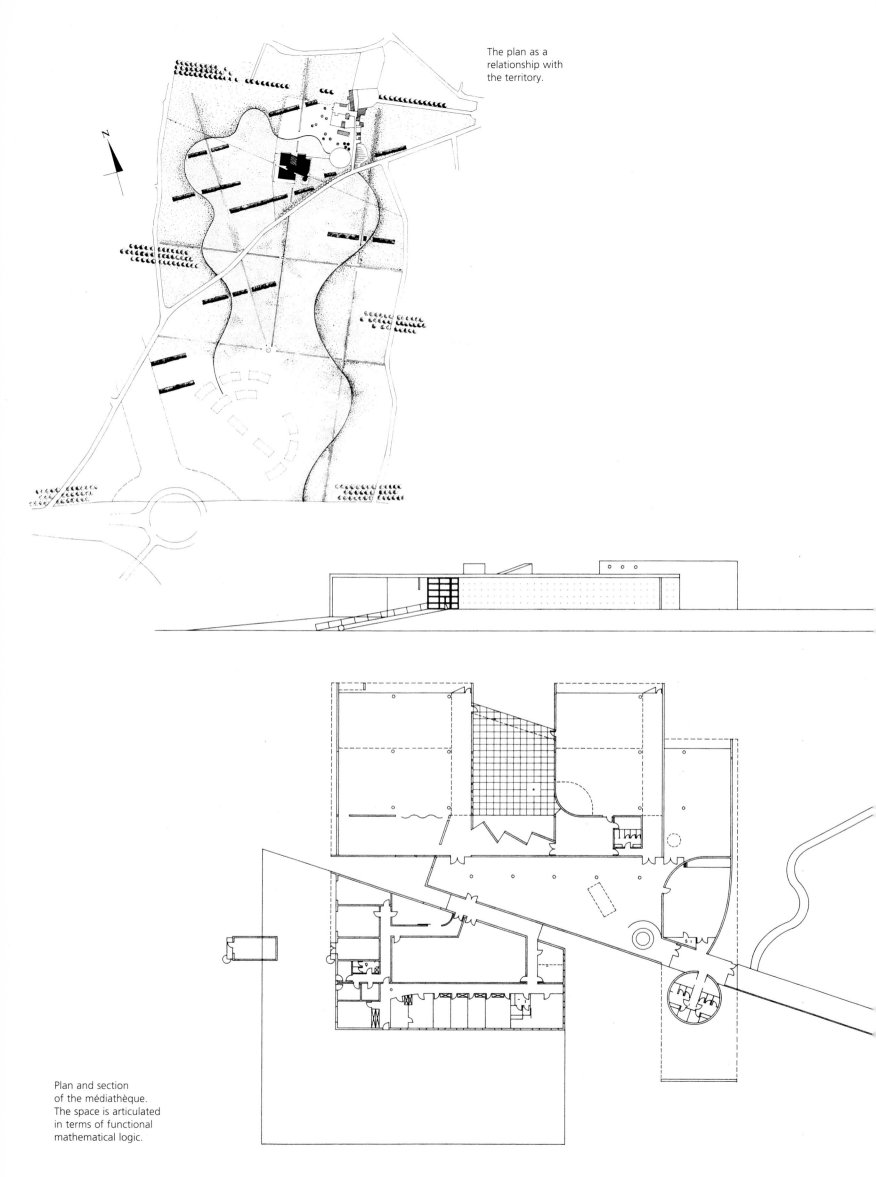

The plan as a relationship with the territory.

Plan and section of the médiathèque. The space is articulated in terms of functional mathematical logic.

Axonometric projection
and axonometric
vertical sections for
verifying the inclination
of the plan's
foundational axis.

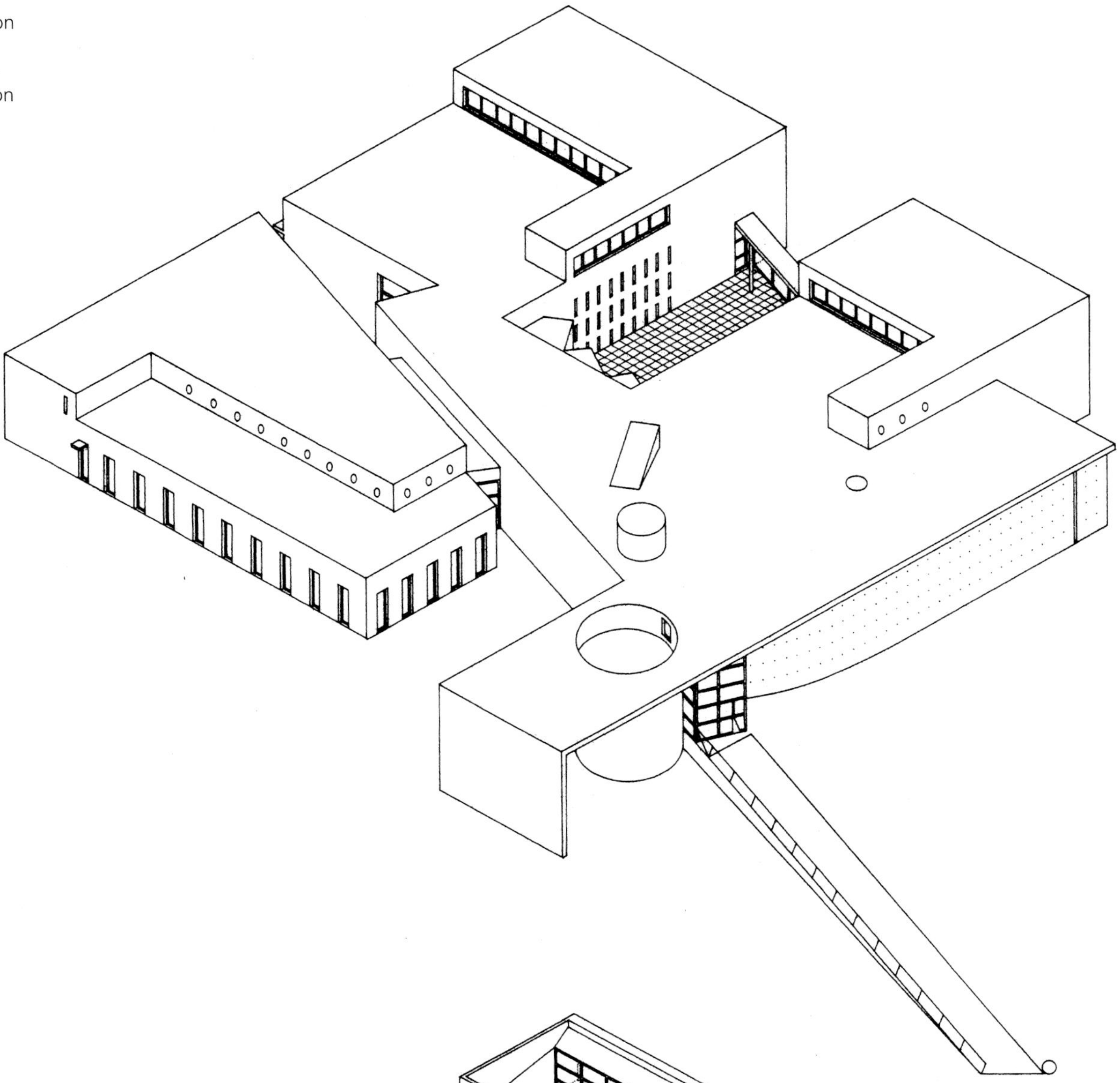

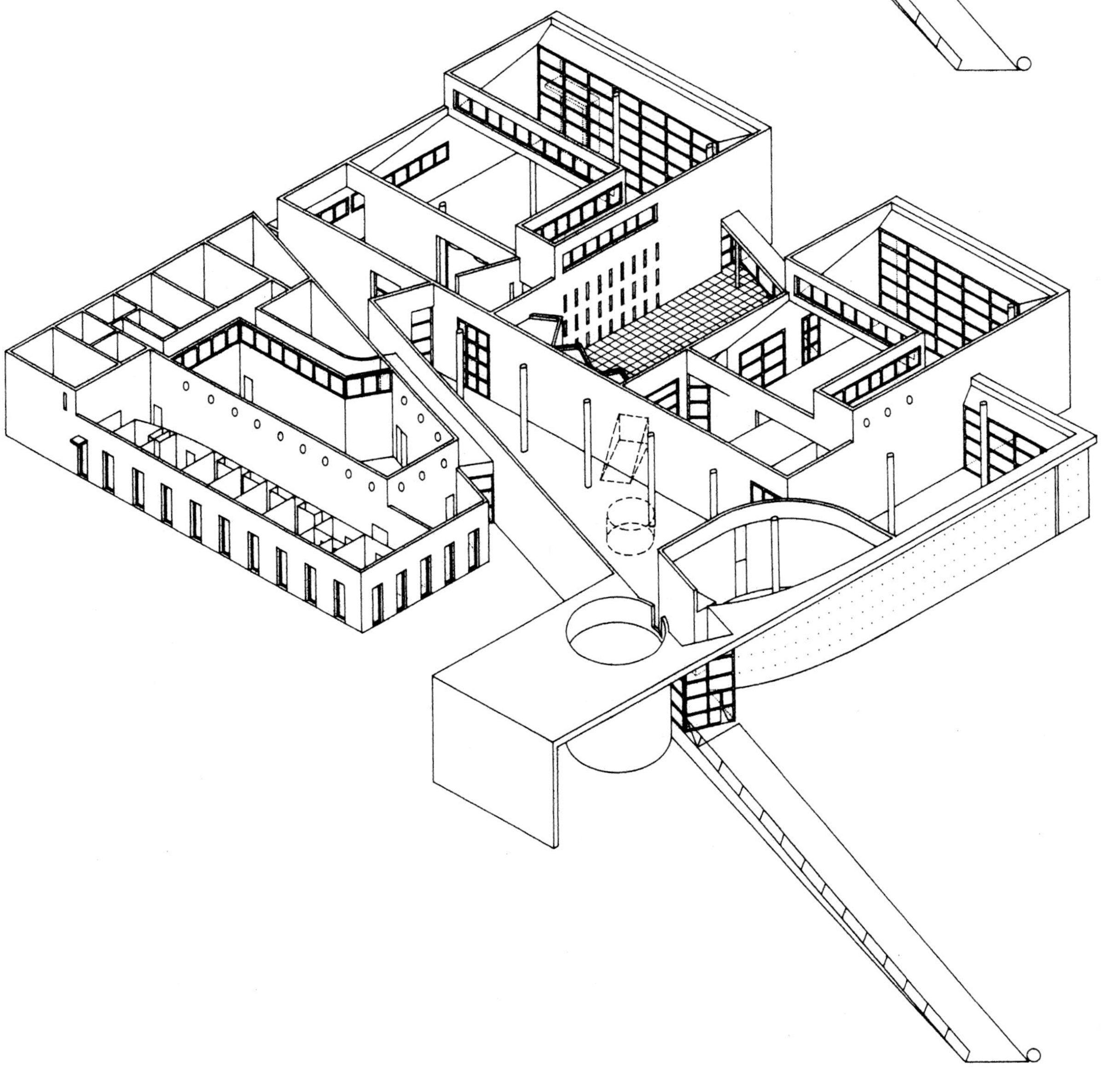

"Valère Mathé"
Professional Institute
Olonne sur Mer, 1992

Architectonic idiom becomes part of the composition of surfaces.

Planned as a Hotel School, this building rises on the outskirts of Olonne sur Mer.

Also in this case, Jean-Claude Pondevie has concentrated on a plan that is suggestive of the rustic architecture of the zone, bathed in sunlight. The white of the walls, the large horizontally running glass walls, of which Le Corbusier and Giuseppe Terragni were so fond, reveal the influence of the rationalist school, but also a precise reference to the environment. As always Pondevie tried to reconcile tradition and modernity in order to obtain rigorous functionality and high formal quality, which are the true signs of good architecture.

The organization of the interior spaces is in line with the standards of school architecture: the classrooms on the north side, the kitchens, offices, confectionary and facilities in the central zone, and the entrance hall, bar and two restaurants open to the public along the front on the street. There is no want of a "model" room and there is also a multifunctional hall at the service of the whole complex.

The panoramic opening of the southern facade, which looks on the playing fields situated on the other side of the road, is equipped with large sun-breakers in order to avoid the risk of overheating during the summer period.

The school ground-floor plan describes the connection and continuity of spaces and functions.

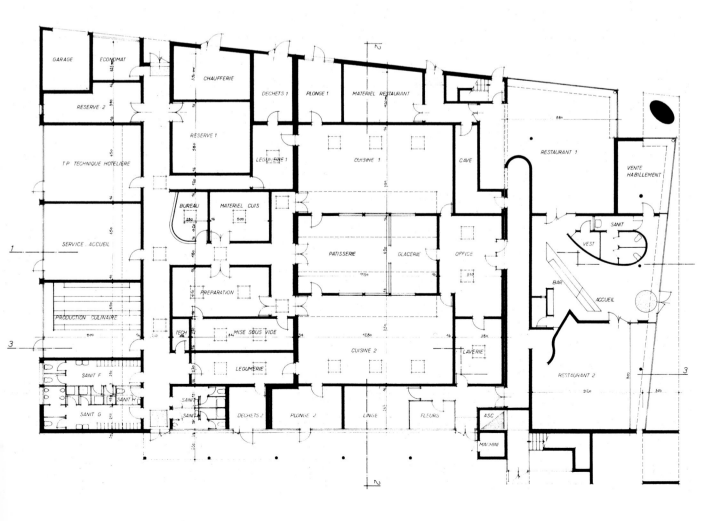

Carefully considered and articulated functionalism is the mark of Pondevie's work.

The choice of a strong element is in this case a recollection of the Doric pillar.

The interior as the
sense and continuity
of the discourse
of a plan.

The Specialized Hospital Centre
La Roche sur Yon, 1993

This small scholastic complex was designed to receive children in the course of their treatment at the psychiatric hospital of La Roche sur Yon. The building was planned for the inside of the "open" perimeter of the Hospital Centre, in a green clearing, and it substituted the pre-existent prefabricated constructions.

In planning this, Jean-Claude Pondevie had to take into account existing data and obligations, such as access, recreational space, orientation, the possibility of the extension of a class and so on. The complex comprises four classes and the director's office, which all open on the area chosen for recreation.

The perimetric facade of the real school rooms faces south, and is therefore amply glass-walled and protected by a brise-soleil.

The studio and the meeeting room, at some distance, have been organized along a separate body open at both ends.

Particular importance has been given in this work to illumination by daylight and to protection of the means of access.

The theme of the project, which unites education, medicine and environment, combines these elements in a space suitable for satisfying all the requirements that its particular function presents. The quiet effect of Pondevie's architecture, consisting of white walls and transparencies is, besides, quite able by itself to offer serenity to special users. By far the most important thing here is the attention given by the planner to the human scale of the architecture and to its tone of warm welcome.

The function of spaces is the starting point for the functional articulation of the forms.

Curve and line stand out in axonometric projection.

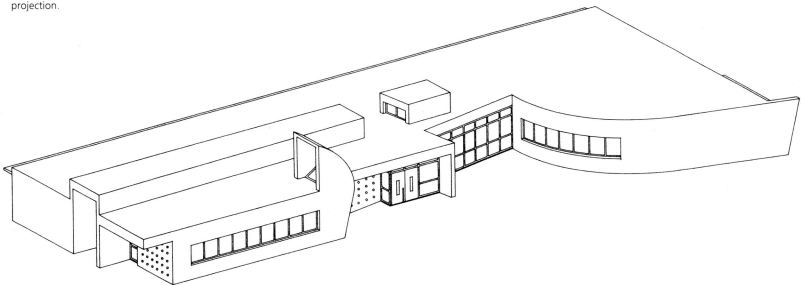

Architectonic
confirmation becomes
even more evident
when the optical cone
widens.

Plans, sections
and perspectives
highlight the process
of planning and
underscore functional
and mathematical
discourse.

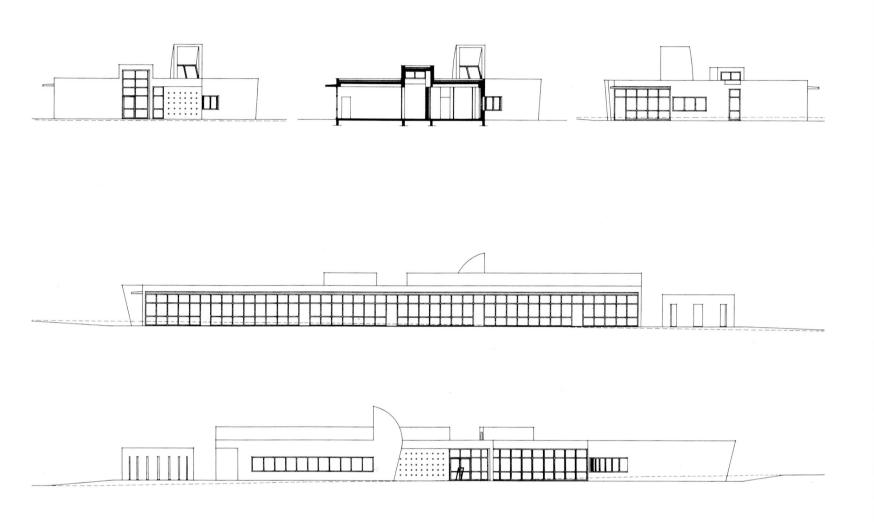

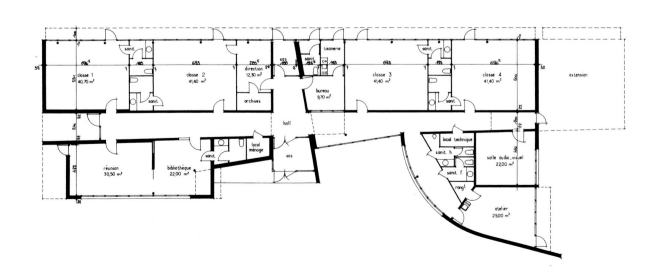

General view and the
details of the rear view
are the vision of the
rules and number.

"Paul Langevin" College
Olonne sur Mer, 1993

Perspective design as a check on the development of a plan.

The geometry of orthogonal projections of the perspective and the section are the most precise way possible of controlling the scanning of the project.

Provision had been made for the construction of this building, a boarding school for 500 students, along a street with heavy traffic in town, which means that it will have to be integrated with the pre-existent urban fabric. While researching his project, Jean-Claude Pondevie decided to impose a rigorous, almost metallic, and above all, white architecture, so as to make it a point of reference for the whole panorama of the town. This constitutes a way to confer a precise identity on the zone.

Moreover, the relationship between the interior and exterior as represented clearly announces the function of the complex.

The architecture expressed by this project seems to be very complex. Peripherally, each facade is differentiated from the others by its verticality, and here the whole is crowned by the overhang of the roofing. The pinnacle on rue Chateaubriand, which is very elaborately sculpted, serves to strongly signal the presence of the construction; and the same task falls to the "attic", which can be seen from a distance, owing to its wooden screen.

There is a quite evident rejection, here, of facile and decorative forms, and the search for a strong, timeless form expressed with the rigour with which every element has been worked out.

More than ever, the colour of the building should recall the white of the Vendée and the light of the *côte de lumière*. These are the elements that identify this work of architecture which, thanks to them, will stand out in its surroundings, but without overwhelming them.

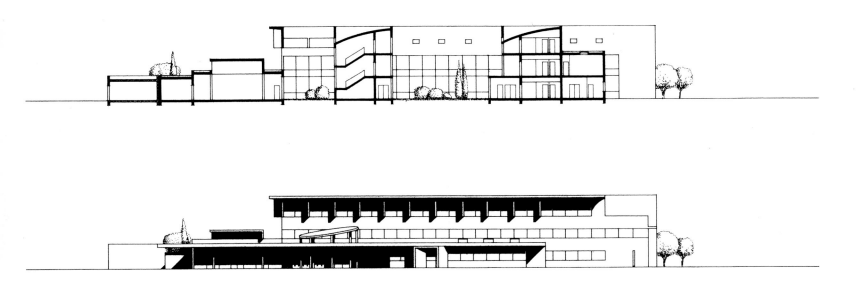

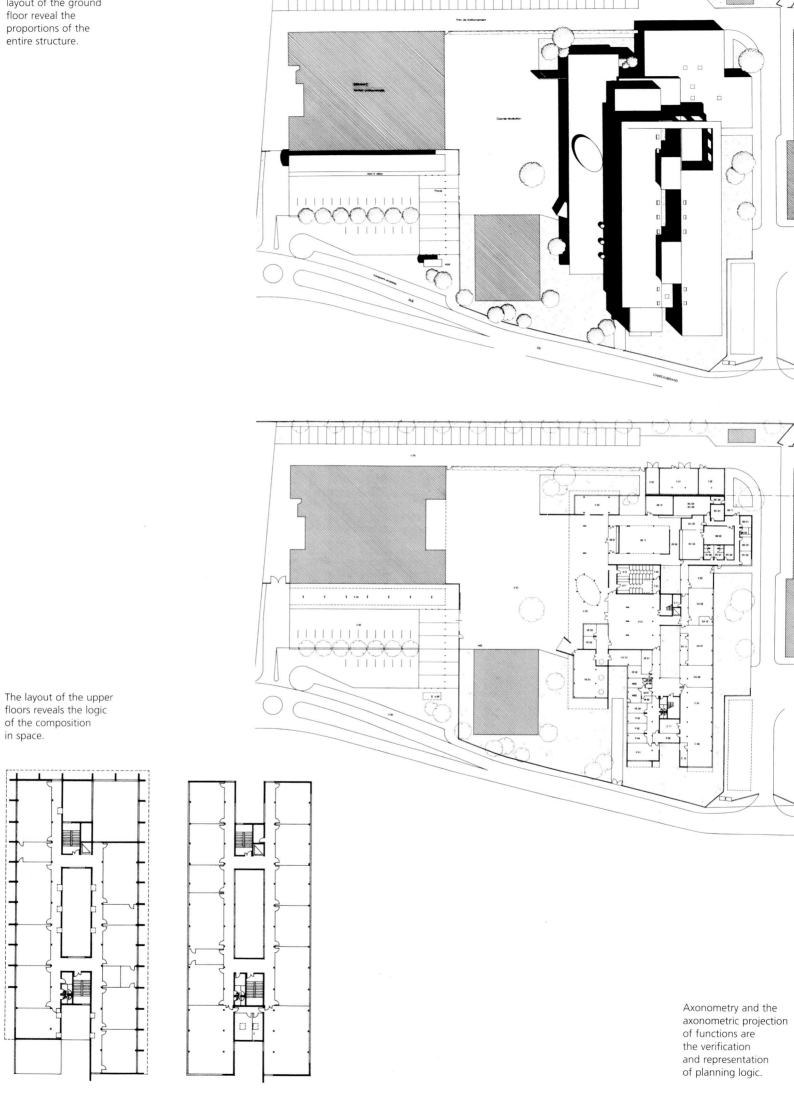

The planimetry and layout of the ground floor reveal the proportions of the entire structure.

The layout of the upper floors reveals the logic of the composition in space.

Axonometry and the axonometric projection of functions are the verification and representation of planning logic.

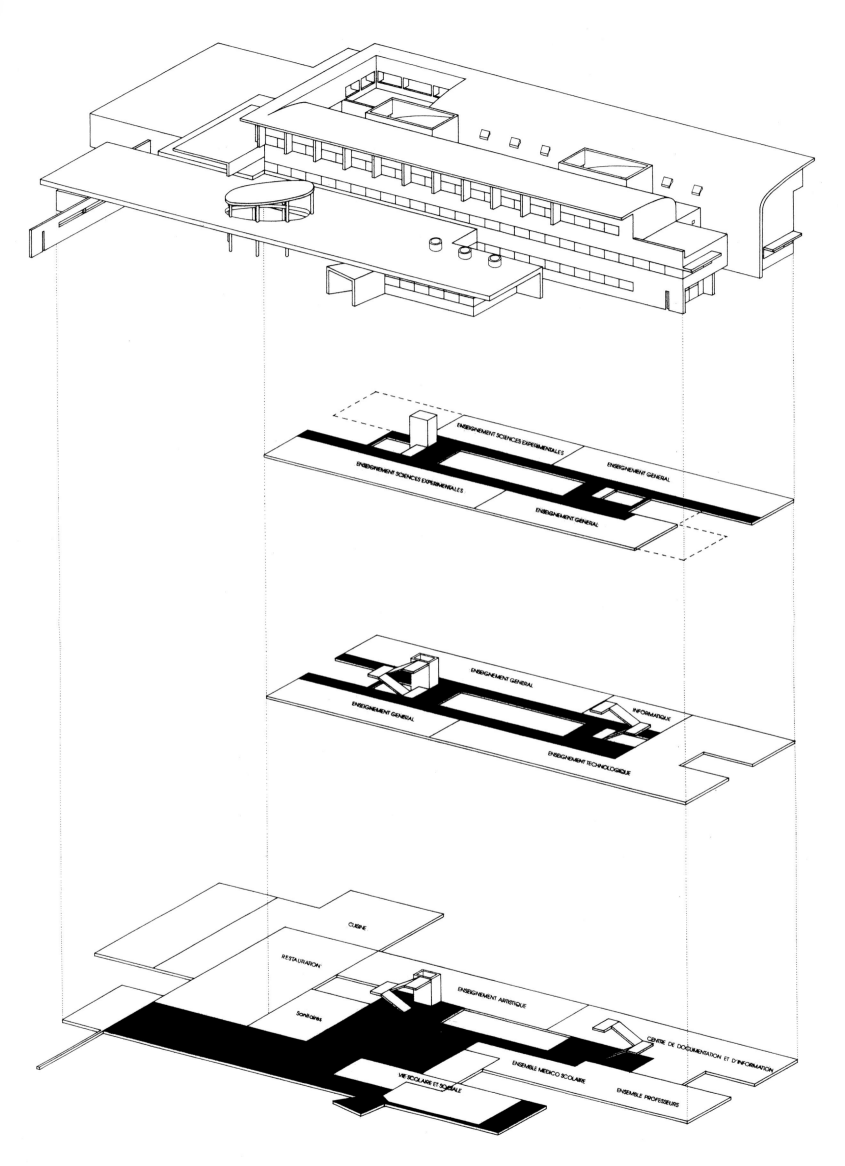

ENSEIGNEMENT SCIENCES EXPERIMENTALES

ENSEIGNEMENT GENERAL

ENSEIGNEMENT SCIENCES EXPERIMENTALES

ENSEIGNEMENT GENERAL

ENSEIGNEMENT GENERAL

INFORMATIQUE

ENSEIGNEMENT GENERAL

ENSEIGNEMENT TECHNOLOGIQUE

CUISINE

RESTAURATION

Sanitaires

ENSEIGNEMENT ARTISTIQUE

CENTRE DE DOCUMENTATION ET D'INFORMATION

ENSEMBLE MEDICO SCOLAIRE

VIE SCOLAIRE ET SOCIALE

ENSEMBLE PROFESSEURS

СТРЖЕМИНСКИЙ

САМУ

Musée des Beaux Arts
Nantes, 1993

The circular interior of the museum's central body is the sense of how the architectonic space of the entire structure is articulated.

The axonometric projection evidences the relationship with all the elements making up the museum.

The value of a museum lies in what it contains, and the form of its space draws its inspiration as a plan from the works that it exhibits. Jean-Claude Pondevie is well aware of this dictate of architecture, and for the "L'Avant-Garde Russe 1905-1925" exhibition presented at the Musée des Beaux Arts of Nantes, for example, he supervised the organization of the spaces so that the visitor might retrace the phases of a particular period in the history of art not only through the works, but also thanks to the particular conformation of their architectonic container.

It is not for nothing that Pondevie turned back to the Suprematism of Malevic, to the work of El Lissitsky, and to Russian Constructivism to create an enviroment in which the dialogue between the work on view and the exibition structures might quicken.

This appears to be even more significant if one knows that the exhibit was hosted in a Museum of a neoclassical layout, and that consequently the architectonic operation had to mediate between a courtly tradition and an avant-garde which has radically renewed art and thrust it unceremoniously into modernity.

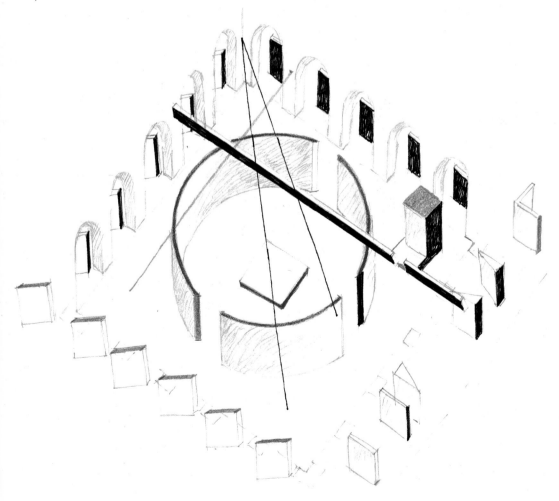

The curved baffle
separator chosen for
the rhythmical
articulation of space.

The description
of forms and functions
follows the idiom
chosen for the
architectonic plan.

ВАРА СТЕПАНОВА НАДЕЖДА УДАЛЬЦОВА АЛЕКСАНДР ВЕСНИН

МИХАИЛ ЛЕ-ДАНТЮ РОБЕРТ ФАЛЬК ИЛЬЯ МАШКОВ СО

Spaces intersect in their interior to facilitate the functional requirements of the museum exhibit.

The foundational
elements of the
museum.

Leglas House
Les Sables d'Olonne, 1994

The desecration of functionality in an unnatural sign.

The interior described with general planimetry.

This residence is situated in the little town of Les Sables d'Olonne, which rises near the seaside in an urban fabric densely filled with small constructions. The town is traversed by narrow lanes but, on the side of the beach, it is overlooked by buildings of from six to eight storeys.

It was in this kind of context that Jean-Claude Pondevie created a private home that celebrates, with considerable style, family unity and its privacy. Accordingly, the building is organized around a small garden, which in some way separates it from the surrounding ones. A small courtyard connects the closed with the open space, in this way making it possible for the architecture to be articulated round volumes in which "man is the measure".

Pondevie's disposition of volumes enables the Leglas House to respect the continuity of the urban fabric of the zone. The terrace roofing, overlooked by the taller constructions, accommodates a hanging garden, and the architectonic solutions facilitate the integration of the structure with the surroundings.

The white-painted walls, the small details in the punctuation of the railing, the drip moulding, and the loopholes are so many details that justify the emphasis put on the formal, almost mathematical, intentions of this work of Pondevie's.

Axonometry as the descriptive idiom of the project.

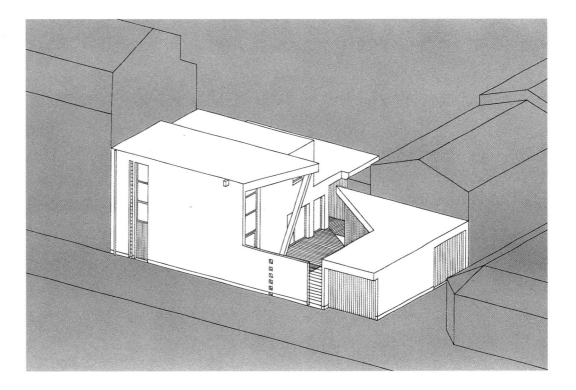

The plan of the upper floor.

Bottom small and large signs of Pondevie's functionalism.

The plan of the ground floor.

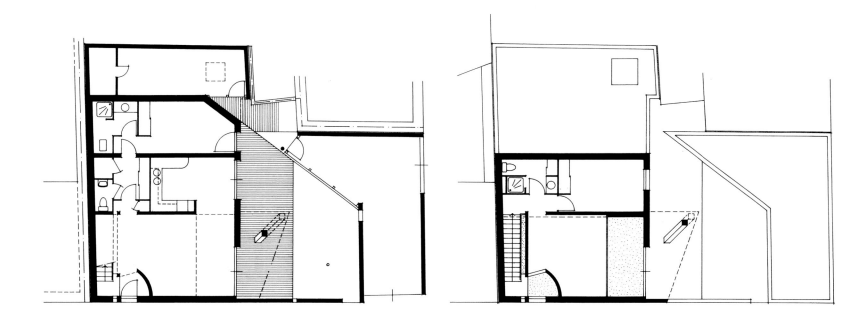

Sections are
the representation
of the assembled
interior space as a view
of the relationship
between form
and function.

A detail becomes
the quality of the work
of architecture.

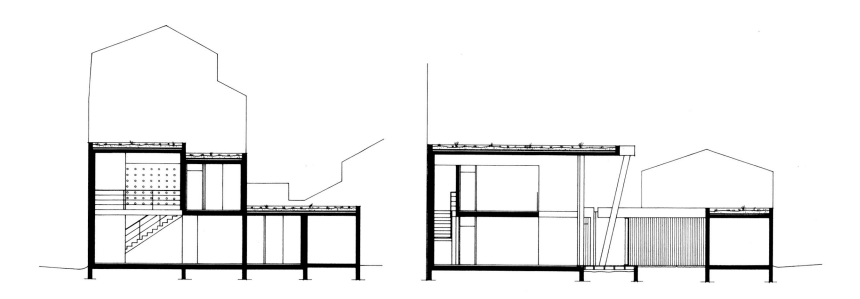

Le Musée du Vignoble du Pays Nantais
Le Pallet, 1994

An out-of-scale element as a hymn to functionalism.

This museum, built at Le Pallet, a village in the province of Nantes, was designed to contain and preserve old agricultural equipment and tools used in vine cultivation.

One gains access to the museum by way of a panoramic parking area. On the left, a projecting body serving as a belvedere rises on the building and opens on the valley. The roofing of the construction is covered with vegetation, which ensures its continuity with the natural environment. Also the use of stone facing confers on the museum complex a feeling of harmony with the sense of tradition and history expressed by the pieces preserved inside.

In this work Jean-Claude Pondevie has designed an image that is at once modern and rustic, an image that is lengthened in the organization of the interior spaces, thanks to the use of raw materials like cement flooring, iron or wooden structures, and so on.

In this way work and nature have found their synthesis. With his usual skill Pondevie made use of bricks, white walls, the arrangement of volumes around the axis of the entrance, a cantilevered-style portal, and of other elements capable of enhancing the functional vigour of his architecture. The architectonic reference thus becomes evident, and expresses the deep sense of an ancient activity carried out in the heart of the French countryside.

Functionalist signs in the territory as a relationship with nature.

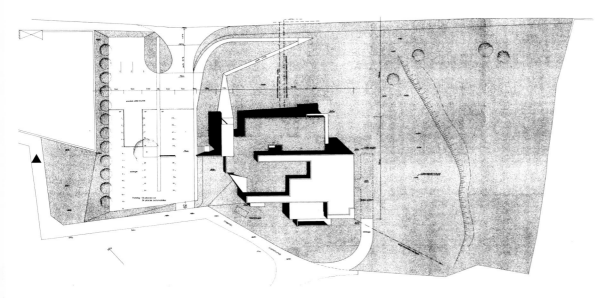

Earth and architecture: continuity between nature and artifice.

Two views that describe the functionalism of the operation.

The plan is the
description of the
intersecting spaces
of the museum.

The interior space with
its functions is the
justification of its form
and idiom.

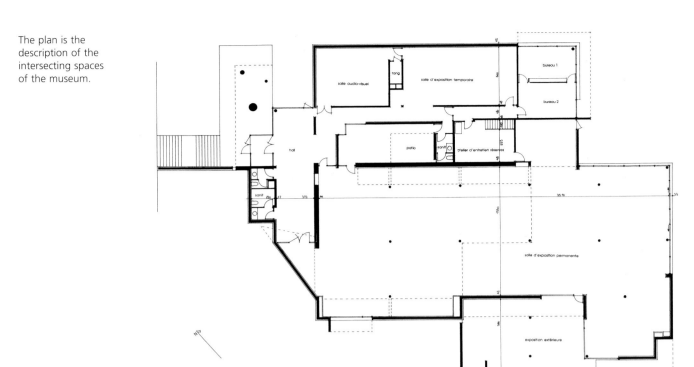

The sections become
a description of how
the space is articulated
in the interior.

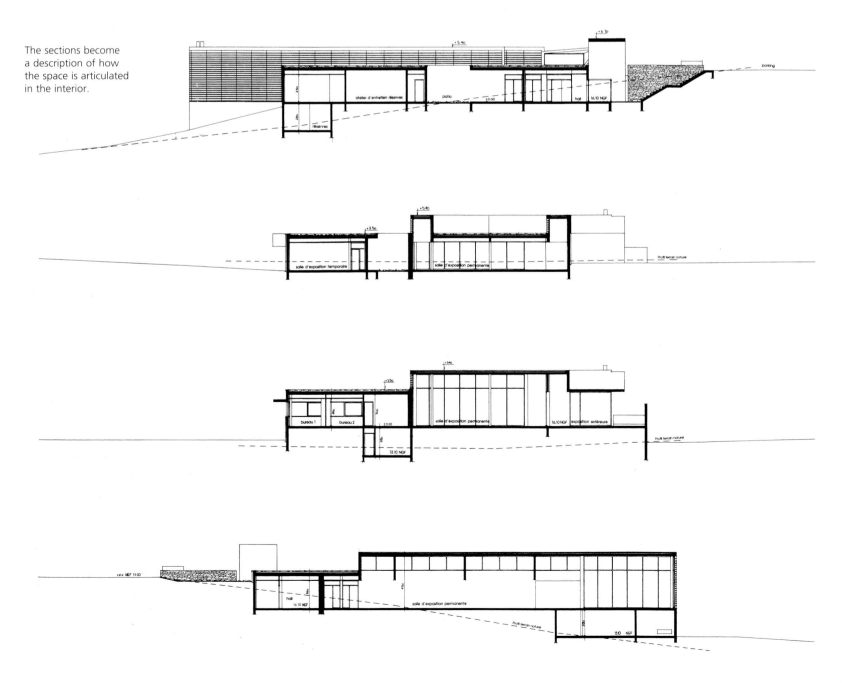

"Milcendeau" Museum
Soullans, 1994

The strength of a form capable of qualifying a work of architecture in relation to its function.

Fullness as strong "silence", as a slight pause in heavy transparency.

The "Milcendeau" Museum is situated only a few kilometres from the village of Soullans in the western zone of the Vendée. Its enlargement, decided in 1991, provided for the restructuring of the entrance and the creation of public sanitary and hygienic facilities, a large hall for permanent exhibitions, rooms for technical studios, and a garage for the guard.

Jean-Claude Pondevie's architectonic solution retains the sober line and minimalist geometric approach that characterize his architecture, but it also brings into play a series of references to history and to the natural environment.

Thus, the play of water in the fountain evokes Milcendeau's stay in Spain, and the large hall for permanent exhibitions is illuminated overhead by the northern light, thanks to a large slit in the roofing, while a projected body serving as a belvedere opens on the lawn.

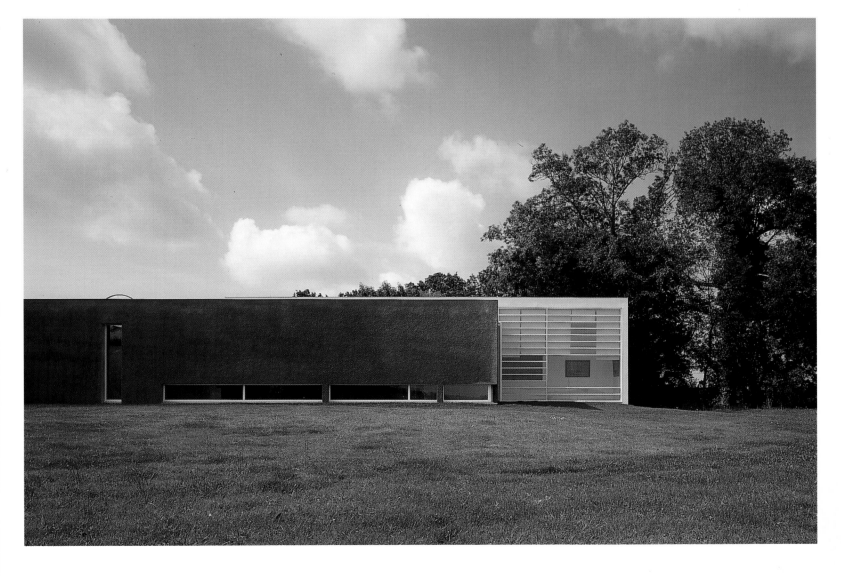

A descriptive
axonometric projection
of the interior
walkways.

One of the interior
corridors revealed
by light.

The plan describes the
distributional idea of
the museum.

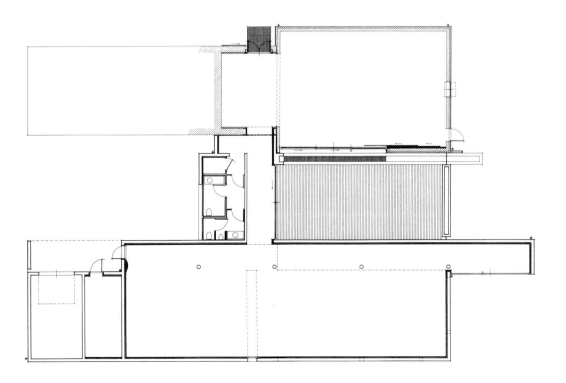

"Le Coteau"
Residential Complex
La Roche sur Yon, 1995

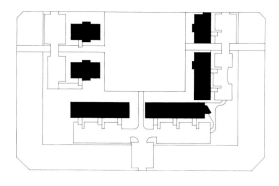

Planimetry as a
rhythmical concept
in the distribution
of volumes.

In this structure Jean-Claude Pondevie demonstrates all his ability to organize volumes and to design an architecture of outstanding importance. This residential complex, in fact, may be seen as nothing less than a synthesis of the history of late functionalism, reconsidered in a contemporary key. The paintings of Piet Mondrian or of Paul Klee emerge plastically in the facades and in the volumes, transforming themselves, in the large white surfaces, into a series of formal punctuations that state a planning philosophy inspired by reason and by a great architectonic culture.

The complex accommodates thirty-eight flats. The planimetric direction of the work obeys the standards set for the development of the zone included in "Zac du Coteau 2", with the buildings situated in the heart of a future quarter of one-family houses. This induced Pondevie to study an arrangement of blocks that would ensure the autonomy of the single lots.

Each building is so orientated that the lodgings are placed on the east-west and north-south axes, so that as much as possible they can benefit from daylight. The complex is equipped with a public parking area and two private parking areas, the latter of which are connected only by an inter-residential lane reserved for pedestrians and cyclists.

Houses support one
another in the diversity
of their ownership.

The relationship of the
complex with exterior
space.

The sequence of
separate lodgings in the
various plans.

The geometry of the
typical facade defining
the project.

The lower plan as a
significant connection
with the upper parts
of the complex.

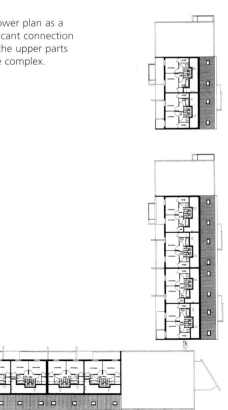

"Parc de la Noue" Residence
Nantes, 1995

The architecture and nature of a residential complex.

A large park crowning a seven-storey building with forty flats; that is the element that characterizes this work planned by Jean-Claude Pondevie.

The park is an extension of the Château de la Noue park, along whose axis the building is orientated. In its architectonic image, however, the construction figures as a sort of "piece of sculpture" deposited on the lawn.

Here, with great rigour, Pondevie takes full advantage of his planning philosophy, organizing the facades with an unfaced brick walling and deliberately leaving white all the other accessory surfaces: balconies, the cantilevered canopies of entrances, window borders, etc.

The building presents itself as a formally articulated structure, with volumes marked by great plasticity.

The two corner wings placed at right angles enclose a structure vaguely suggesting a dome; and this solution confers on the architecture a dynamism and articulation that break the functionalist rigour of the facades and introduce in a perfectly geometrical design an element of contradiction that brings the work back to its postmodern condition.

The plans of the residential tower, which reveal the mathematical logic governing the distribution of interior spaces.

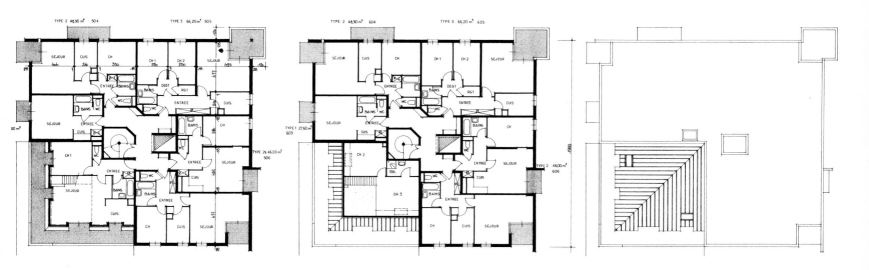

The main perspective,
in which the variations
in the colour of the
material change the
description of the
various architectonic
parts.

An inversion
of architectonic idiom
strengthens the
residential complex
at the back.

The walls of the
building decorated with
overhanging elements
and balconies.

"La Folie Finfarine" Tree House
Le Poiroux, 1995

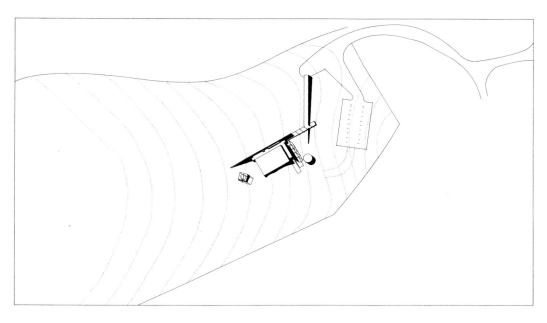

The general planimetry of the tree house, revealing the relationship between the ground and the edifice.

The tree and its "house".

An axonometric projection as a verification of the relationship between an artificial volume and a natural element.

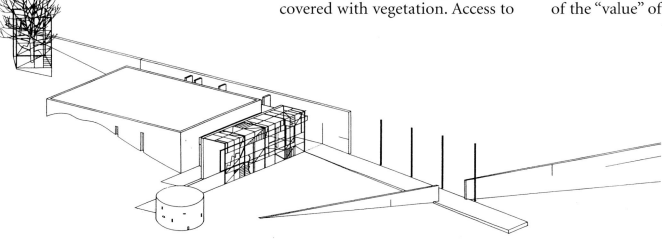

the exhibition room will be provided by a presentation space just before it, orientated on "*La folie*". A small block for the hygienic-sanitary facilities will be open to visitors to the park and museum. The roofing of the building will be covered with green, which is a way of extending the view of the lawn below.

Art and architecture join in a subject of pure creativity and intense planning skill. This work of Jean-Claude Pondevie's intertwines two cultural elements that face and support each other in turn: the functionalist design of the one-family house and the statement of the pure outline of a plan. The two entities fuse in a discourse dense with meanings, from which there emerges the idea of a project that underscores how architecture contrives to find an identity in its true and basic values: the home, greenery, nature, and the environment.

Pondevie opens his design to all possibilities, and exercises his architecture to the full in a rigorous exposition expressing an intuition of the "value" of the plan.

This little work is situated in the interior of a vast natural space in the commune of Poiroux; a sculpture - "*La folie*" - encloses and exalts a fastigial-shaped tree.

On arriving at the parking area, visitors will discover on the lawn this "*folie*" situated above the retaining walls, which form a series of sequences of approach towards the "tree house".

A lobby controls the entrance to the park and to the exposition room, lengthening towards the outside by way of a pergola covered with vegetation. Access to

The earth appears as a matrix: the relationship between the dimension and form of the house and with its surroundings.

The lightness of the functionalist sign reduced to the essentiality of material.

The drawings of the
plans, vertical views
and sections underscore
how the great outdoor
spaces penetrate into
the interior of the
house.

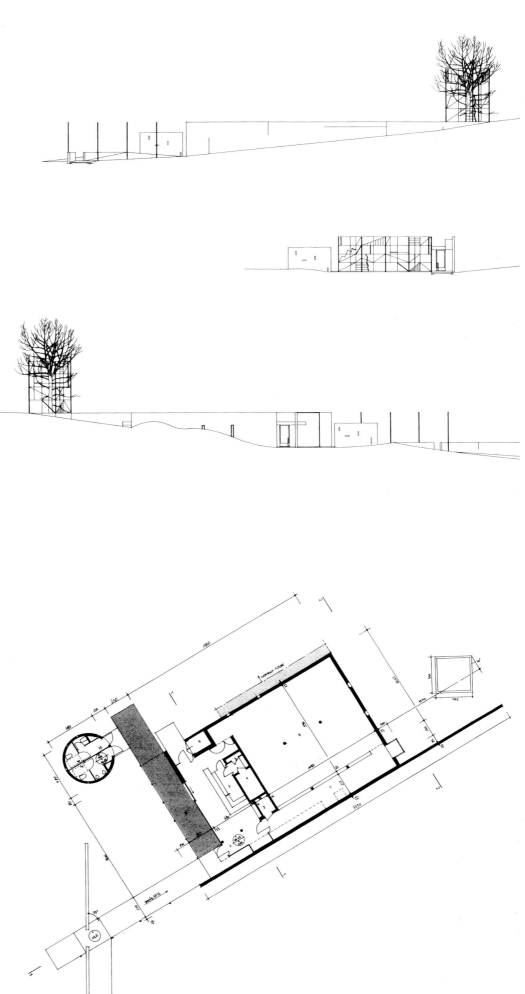

Maison de Brugière
Château d'Olonne, 1996

This one-family house is situated in Château d'Olonne, Vendée, in the heart of a residential quarter of low population density. Originally, the project provided for the creation of a pond and an adjacent swimming pool. Since the construction was to be located in a wooded area, it was to be so oriented as to afford a view of the pond and swimming pool and to give the main rooms full advantage of the sunlight. The entrance to the house leads directly into the living room, which gives access to the kitchen and to the other rooms. The interior spaces have been arranged according to standards of comfort and functionality, their purpose being to create the right atmosphere of cosiness typical of family residences.

The general design of the building is marked by two curved lateral walls, which seem to enclose the internal space in a sort of protective embrace. This curvature favours a harmonious relationship with the natural surroundings and creates the impression that the whole house has been fitted into the depths of the wood. And the oblique line of the roofing, which longitudinally crosses the ellipsoidal cast of the volume, strengthens the balanced dynamism of the whole.

The roofing and the exterior door and window frames are made of natural aluminium and zinc. Wood, however, was utilized for the verandah, which lengthens the living room parquet.

Following his own idiosyncratic conception, Pondevie solves the problem of providing a clear architectonic identity for a construction which, in itself, is a minor work, with nothing imposing about it either in its dimensions or its type. His solution is to fit the residence into a complex geometrical figuration, without however upsetting the quiet image of the whole. This is typical of his designing philosophy, of which this work is a further and significant confirmation.

The architectonic volume and the environment.

The rigour of the
functional geometry
made plastic by the
curvature of the
surfaces.

The cuts of the
openings emphasize
the architectonic
model.

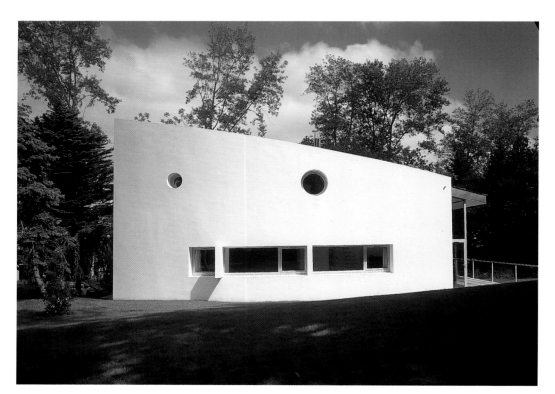

The perspectives relate the proportions of the building.

The plans justify the distributional choice of spaces and functions.

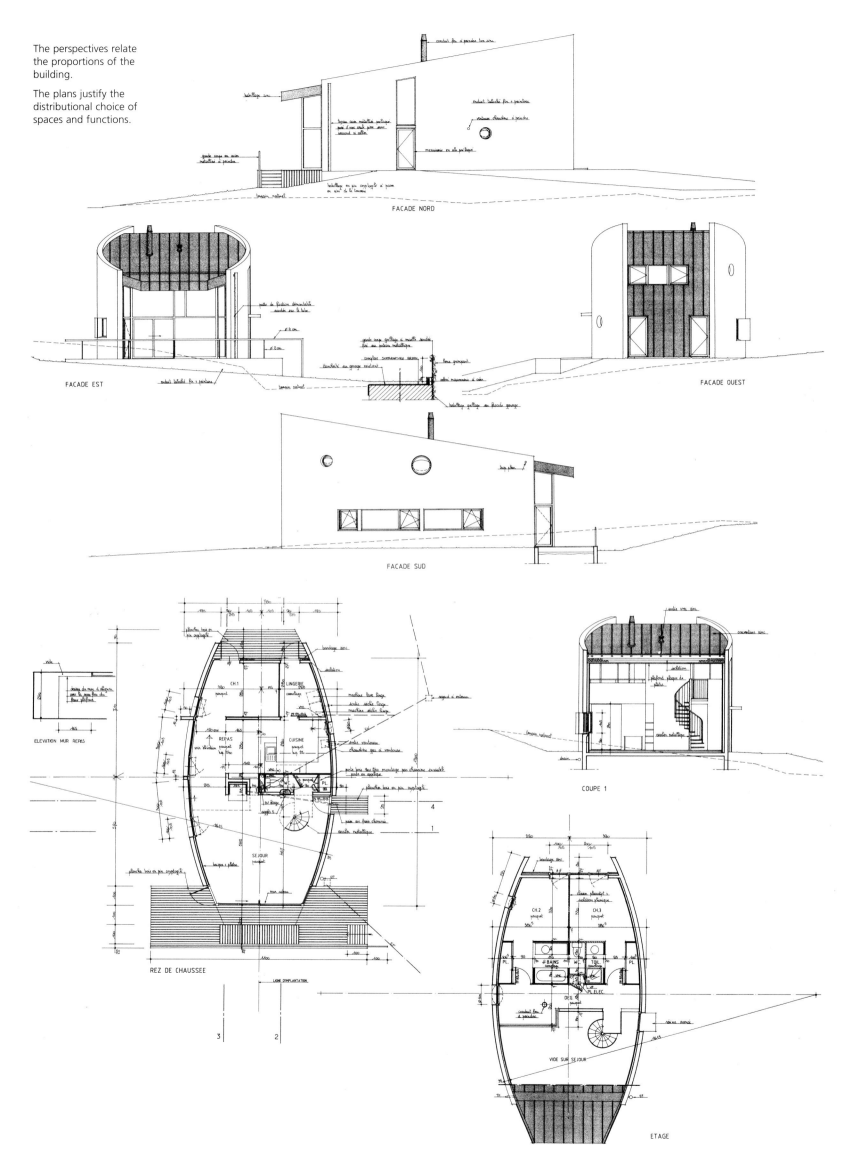

FACADE NORD

FACADE EST

FACADE OUEST

FACADE SUD

ELEVATION MUR REPAS

REZ DE CHAUSSEE

COUPE 1

ETAGE

The sections describe the intermediate geometries of the spaces.

From its interior the entire volume decidedly looks like a true case of architectonic articulation.

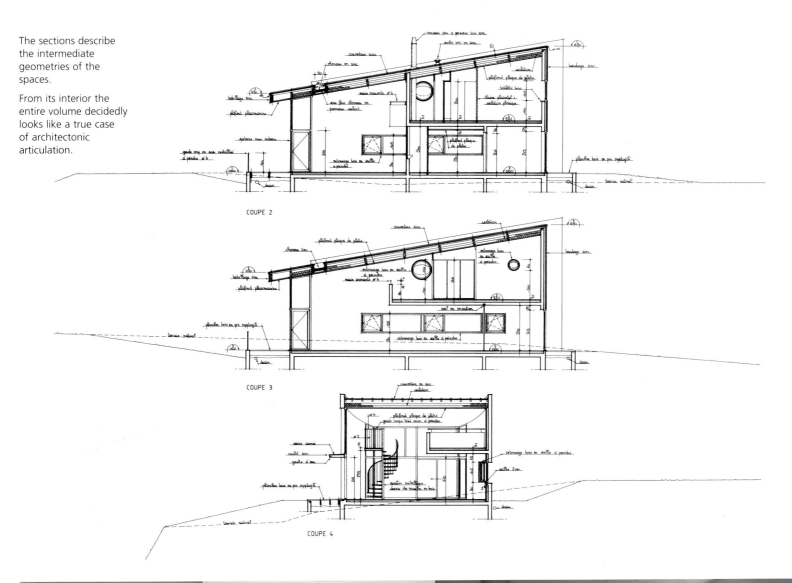

COUPE 2

COUPE 3

COUPE 4

The Town Hall
Le Poiré sur Vie, 1997

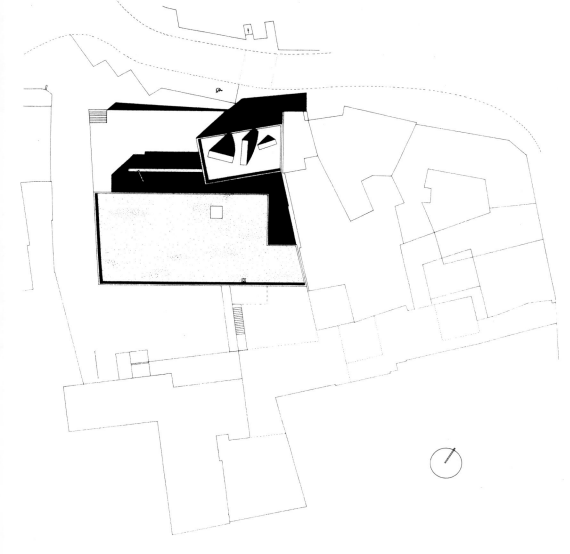

With the project he submitted to the competition for the new Town Hall of Le Poiré, Jean-Claude Pondevie again takes up the forms linked to the tradition of the city.

The market square is situated in the centre of town. Its relatively homogeneous traditional character is punctually obliterated by the garden opening in front of the present Town Hall. The facades of the buildings looking on the square are almost all white or, sometimes, grey. Some of them are in stone. The roofing is in sheet iron or slate.

Pondevie is well aware that he has to deal with a medieval setting. But once again one finds in his project the white of walls, glass surfaces, and brick, all elements with which he makes up a design based on the typical functions of a structure destined to house the offices of a public administration.

The two most important spaces of the entire layout, which are interrelated, are the Council Room and the room set apart for marriages. The other functions, regarding the control of the life of the town, become almost a crowning of the whole work.

"By situating the hall of the Town Council and the marriage room in a continuous relationship with the existing buildings", remarked Pondevie, "we have tried to close and 'complete' the market square, in a way that would partially restore the original shape". Thus, the intention was to propose the new building as an element of integration in the old urban fabric, and at the same time, as an opening to a future that it prefigures.

"On the eve of 2000 shouldn't our projects express and symbolize the creative dynamic of our towns, respecting their traditions and even starting from them and from their architectonic history, which is always a source of inspiration?", Pondevie rightly inquires.

The city and the public building: the relationship between two geometrical natures.

The perspective describes and verifies the imposing presence of the volumes of this building in the urban fabric.

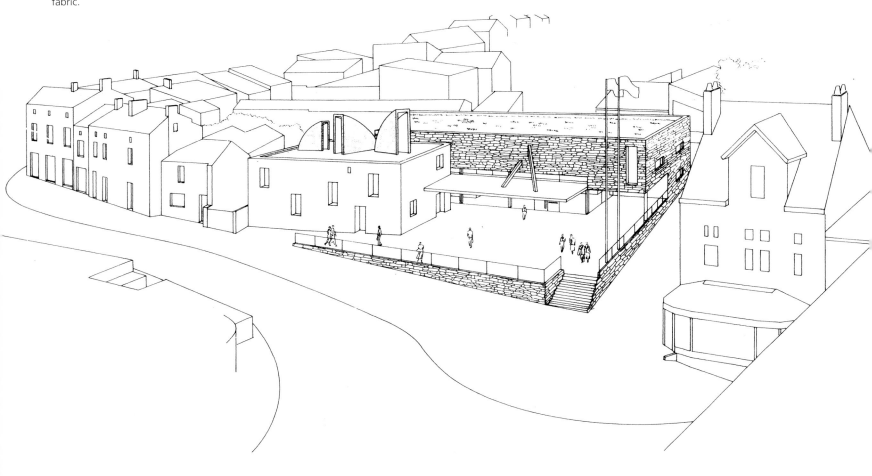

The plan of the upper floor and its connections with the floor below.

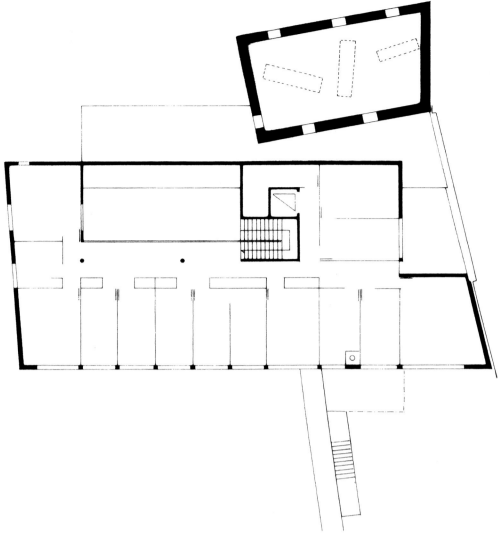

The plan of the ground floor with its public functions.

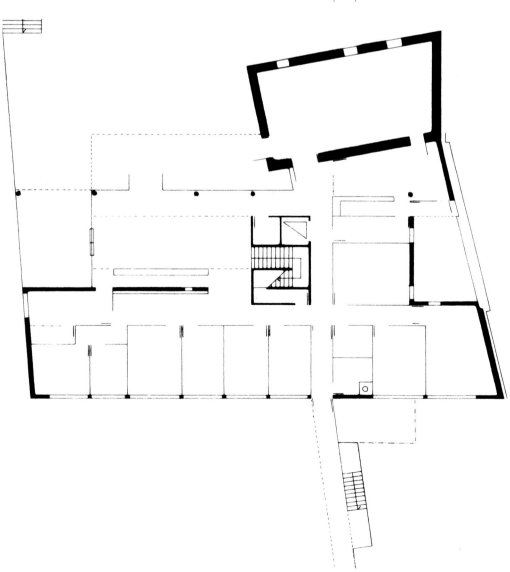

School of Architecture
Tours, 1997

Detail of the project for a School of Architecture which illustrates the punctuation of the volumes with their specific functions.

The project for the new School of Architecture at Tours states some new values in Jean-Claude Pondevie's planning: an unprecedented capacity for modelling facades, a different conception of the entire distributional plan, and experimentation with formal and functional solutions. We find a new kind of research here, fresher, more timely; a research that seems to contain the desire for a verification of his planning philosophy.

The building is to rise in the new Deux Lions quarter, along the two main roads of the town: Avenue Ferdinand Lesseps and rue James Watt. Although it respects all the restraints imposed by the regulations of the Paz de la Zac, the project does not seem to suffer from any sort of constriction This demonstrates once again the great professionalism of Pondevie, who has shown here his capacity for organizing spaces and volumes

according to a dynamic articulation that is quite suitable for a School of Architecture.

Evident here is the close interrelationship that the project establishes with the environment. The studios, which open to the north, are organized into three complexes interrupted by deep recesses. Together with the expositional spaces and the study halls, these studios always remain in contact with the public space. In this way the building expresses its own cultural contents, which considerably differentiate it from the adjacent Law School.

The colour of the facades, the use of fundamental colours that recall those typical of Turenna, and the grafting on of rhythmical punctuations entrusted to panels which have to filter the light in the laboratories, are the new suggestive elements that attribute innovative values to this project compared with Pondevie's previous work. In this regard, the planner speaks of "musical' writing, free openings, a work with vividly coloured dots". It is not a matter of the juxtaposition of simple volumes, but rather the grafting of ancient or classical values on an absolutely modern conception of architecture.

The general site plan reveals the articulation of the spaces and their complex functions.

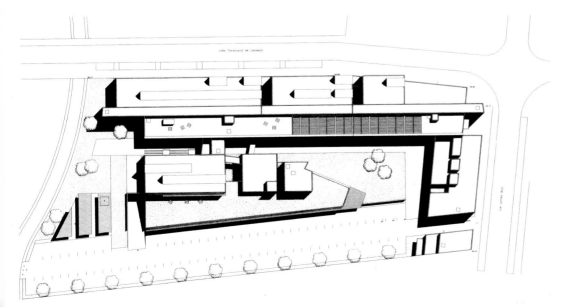

The computer-aided
perspective
representation affords
a view of an articulated
and complex
architectonic whole.

The perspectives
represent Pondevie's
functionalist idiom
modified by
mathematical and
functional logical
approaches.

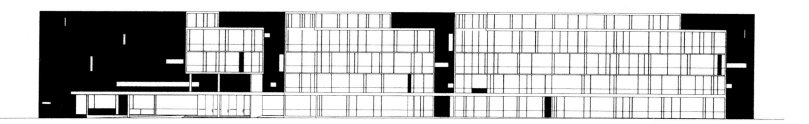

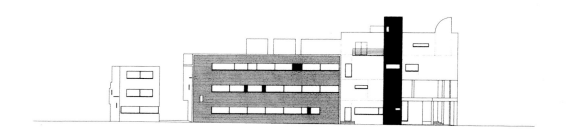

A perspective view always affords new points of view as verifications of the project.

The vertical views state the logical bases of the project, confirming Pondevie's professional rigour.

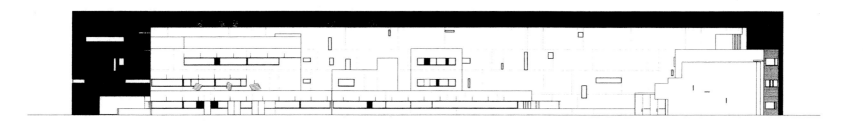

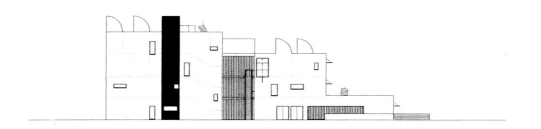

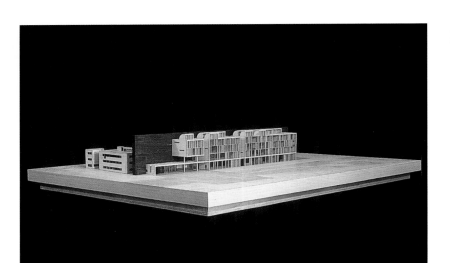

A three-dimensional
view of the project.

The plans of the lower
floors are the bases for
the expansion of the
spaces.

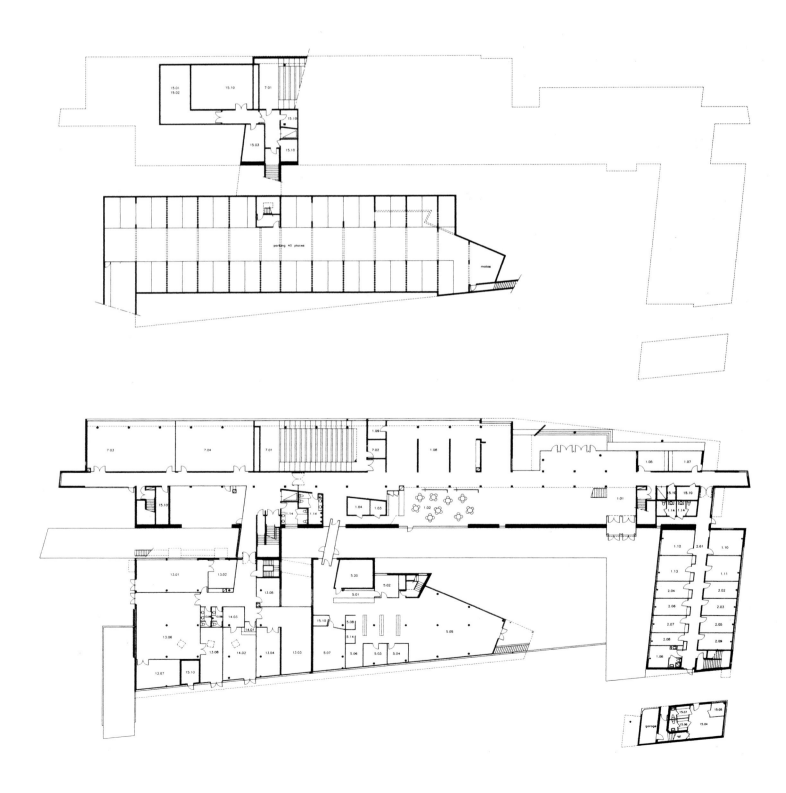

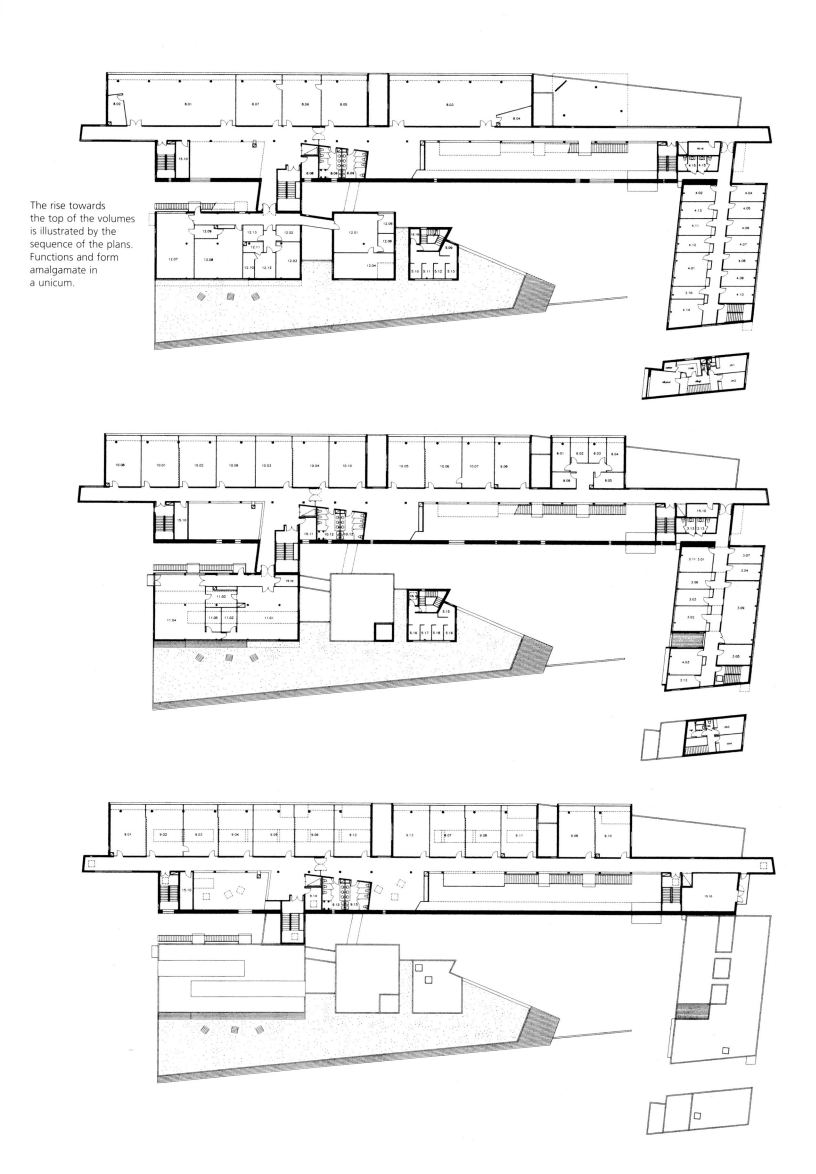

The rise towards
the top of the volumes
is illustrated by the
sequence of the plans.
Functions and form
amalgamate in
a unicum.

Biography

The Jean-Claude Pondevie studio was founded in Paris in 1971. In 1976 it transferred to western France, to La Roche sur Yon, near Nantes.

Jean-Claude Pondevie has always been interested in the plastic arts, and he closely follows developments on the world's artistic scene, outside of which he cannot conceive of architecture. He is also intensely interested in photography, which he practises personally.

He is also an enthusiastic follower of exhibition design, and in 1990 and 1993 he designed the staging of two important shows at the Musée des Beaux Arts of Nantes.

Pondevie has planned a few one-family residences, but only after being assured that the clients knew his works well, and were capable of fully understanding his work. Nevertheless, after many years his work is now essentially carried out in the field of public works, in which he made a name for himself through competitions.

Jean-Claude Pondevie's studio is composed of a dozen people, among whom four architects.